S C H O L A S T I C

LITERA

PLACE

Team Spirit

Copyright acknowledgments and credits appear on page 144, which constitutes an extension of this copyright page.

Copyright © 2000 by Scholastic Inc.   All rights reserved   Printed in the U.S.A.

ISBN 0-439-06141-5

4 5 6 7 8 9 10   09   05 04 03 02 01 00

TABLE OF CONTENTS

Team Spirit

THEME
It's fun to do
things together.

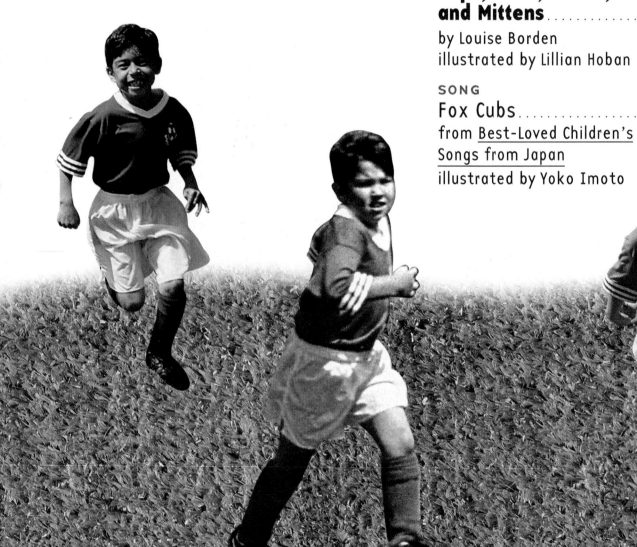

UNIT 3

Team Spirit

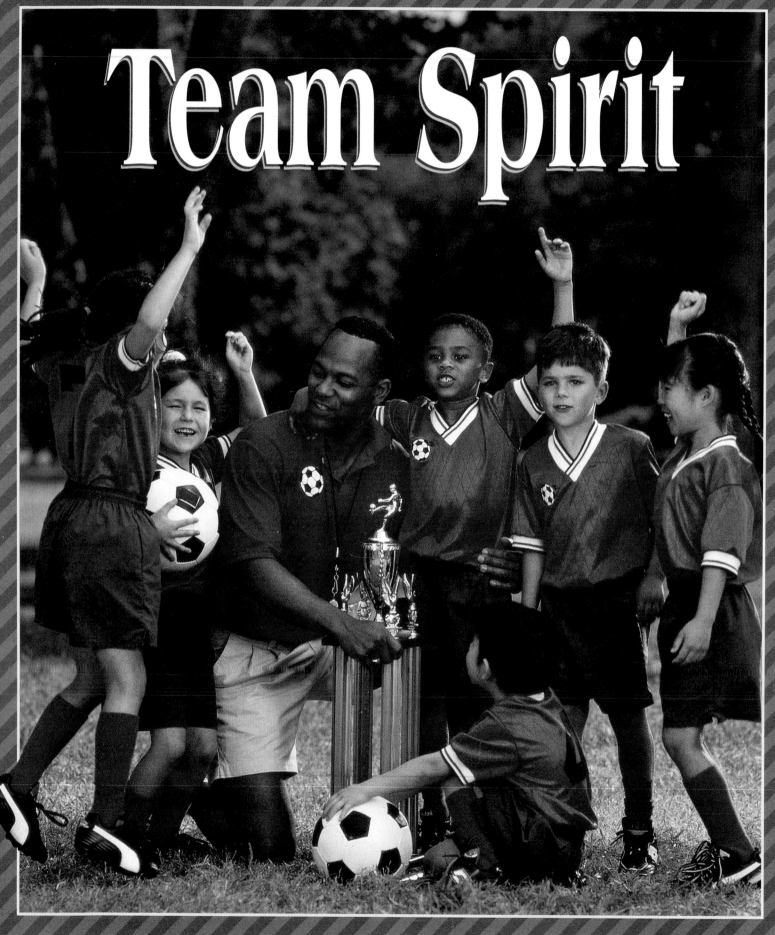

Team Spirit

THEME

It's fun to do things together.

UNIT 3

Welcome to

LITERACY PLACE

Go to a Soccer Stadium

It's fun to do things together.

BET YOU CAN'T

Penny Dale

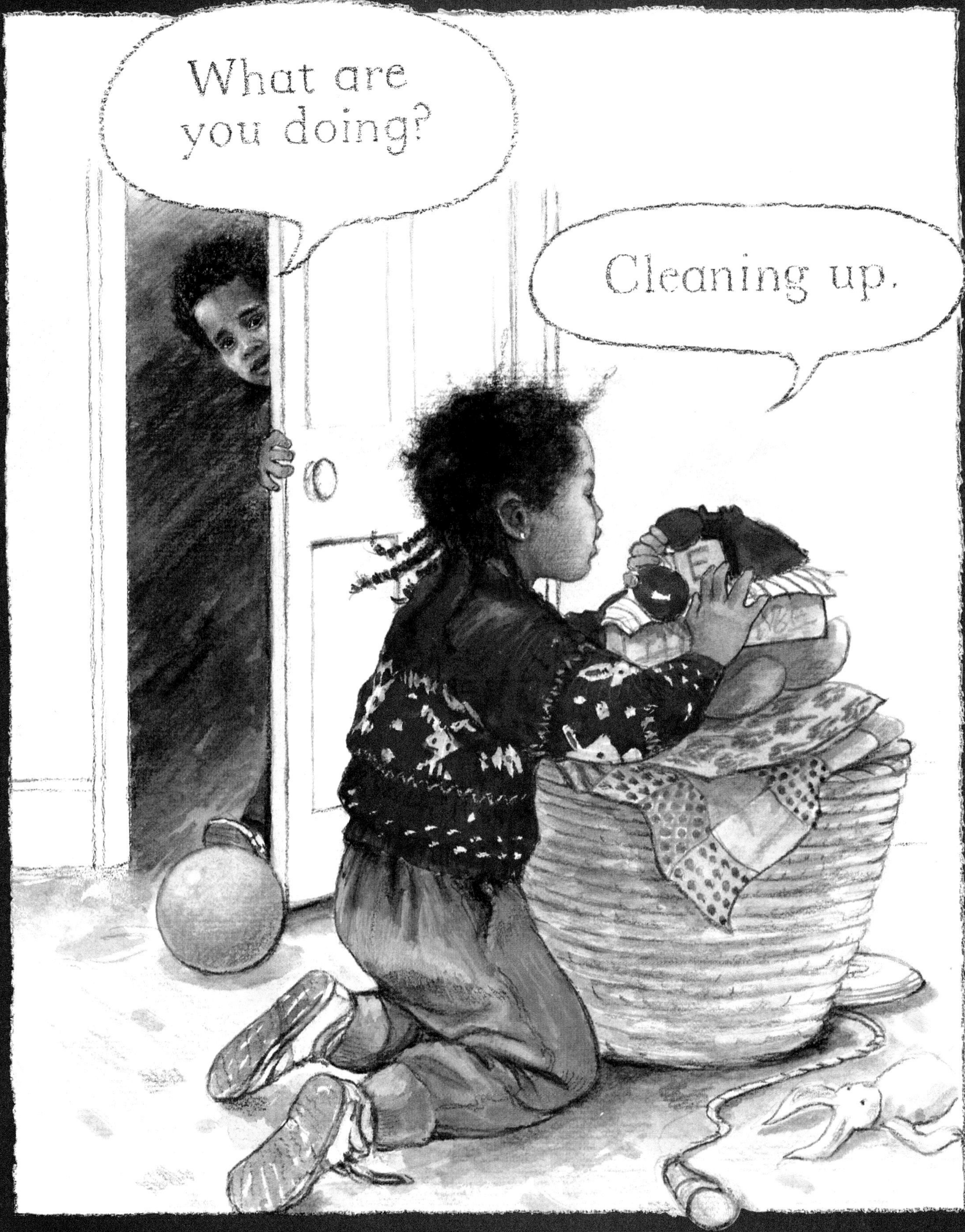
What are you doing?
Cleaning up.

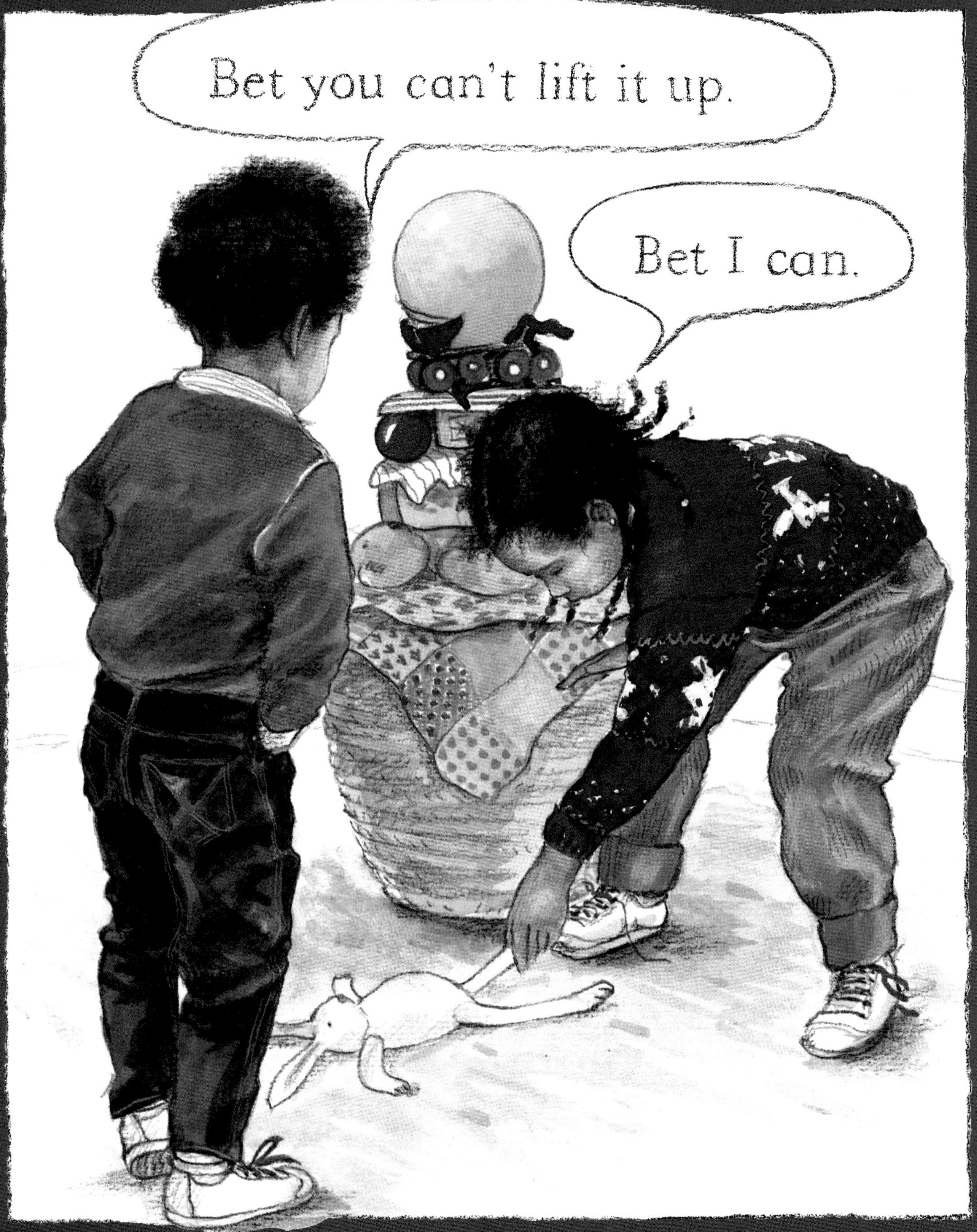
Bet you can't lift it up.
Bet I can.

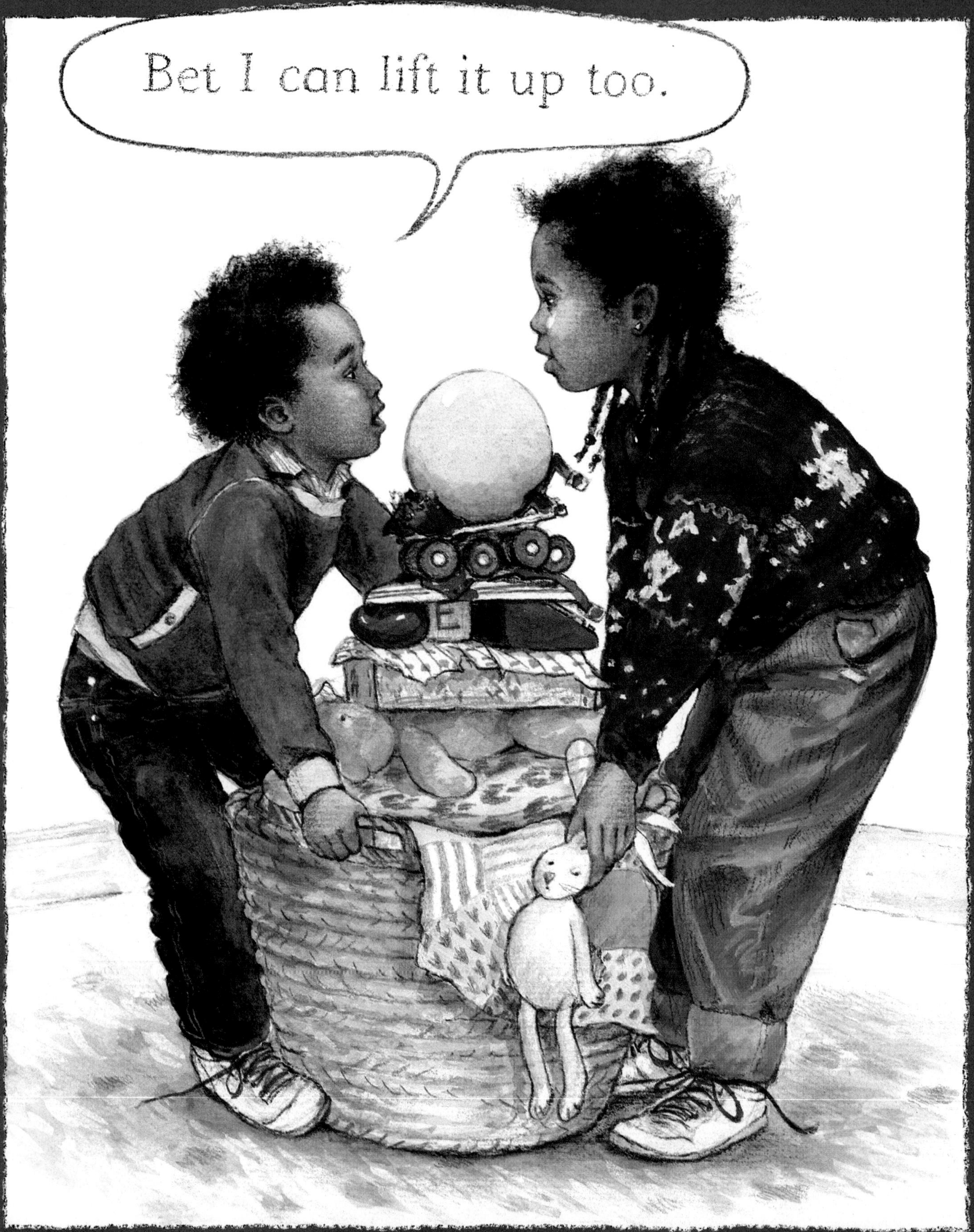
Bet I can lift it up too.

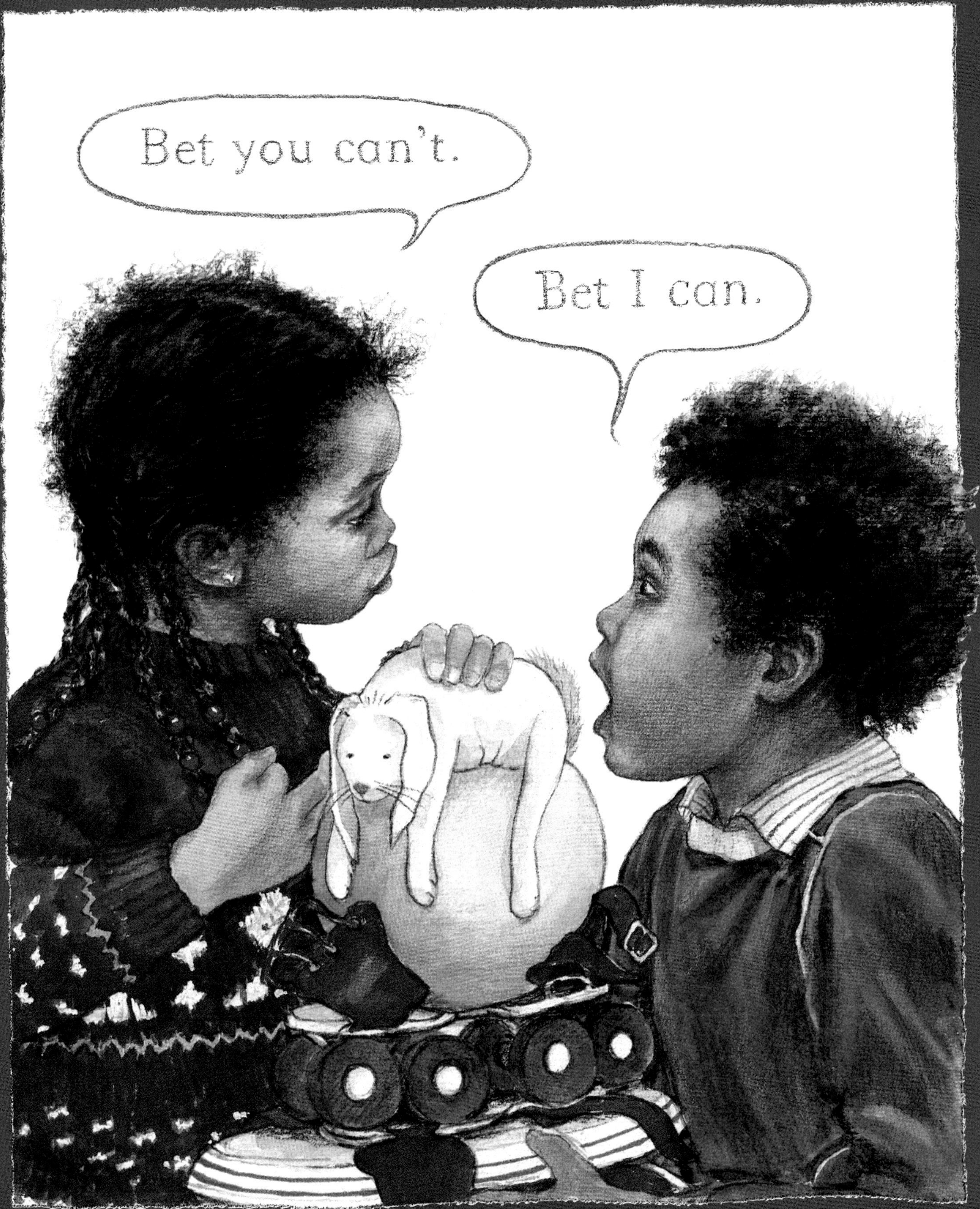
Bet you can't.
Bet I can.

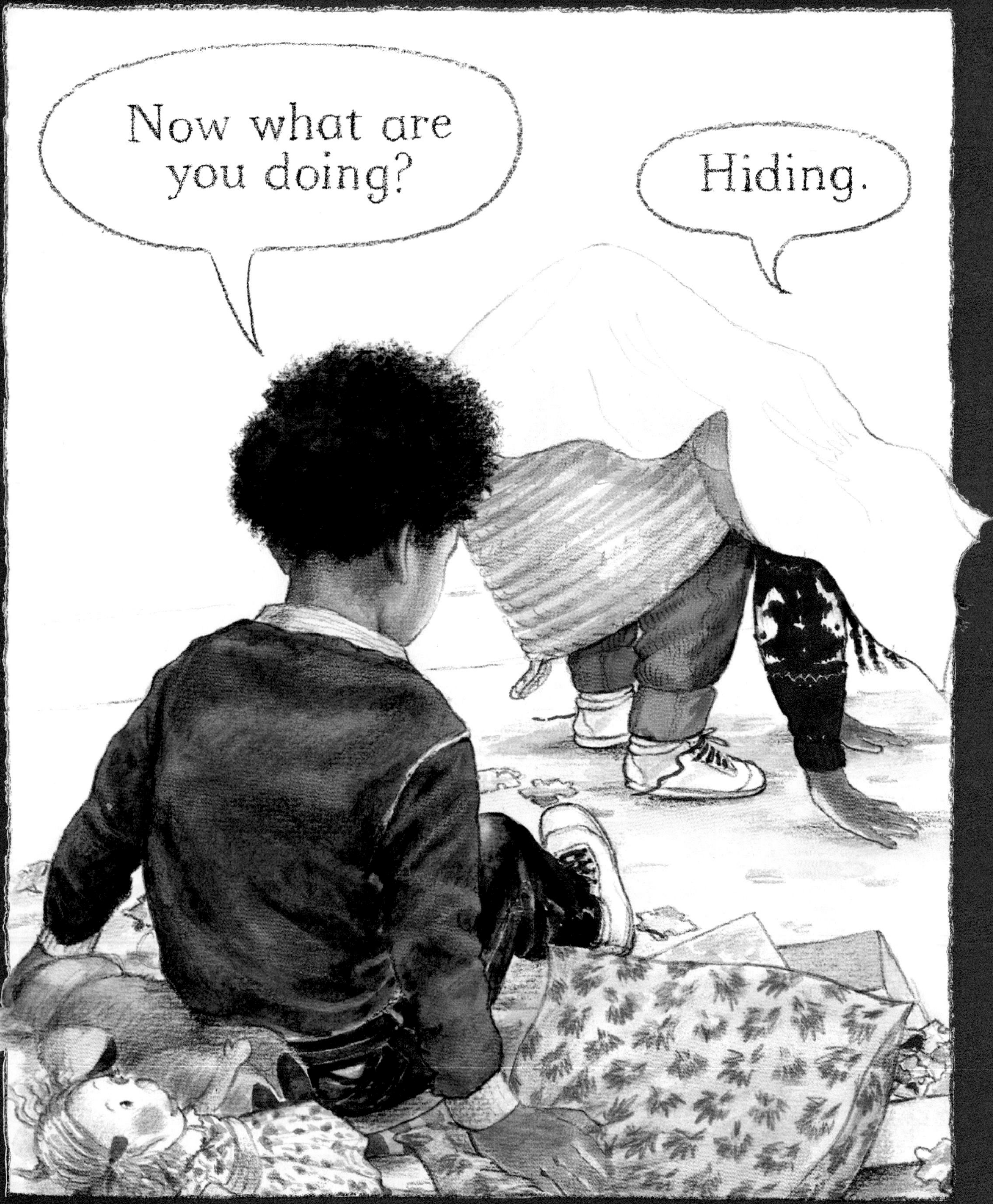
Now what are you doing?
Hiding.

21

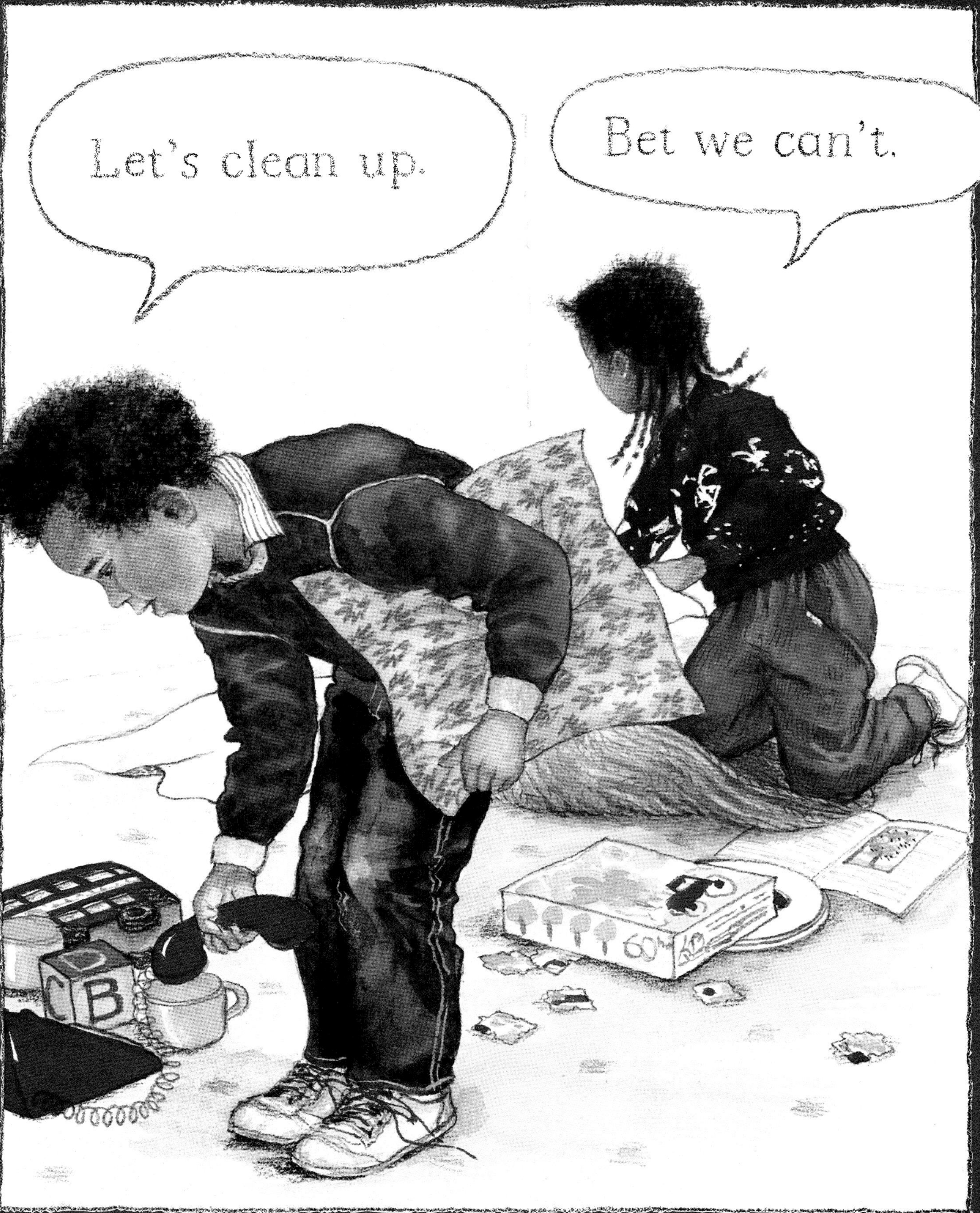
Let's clean up.
Bet we can't.

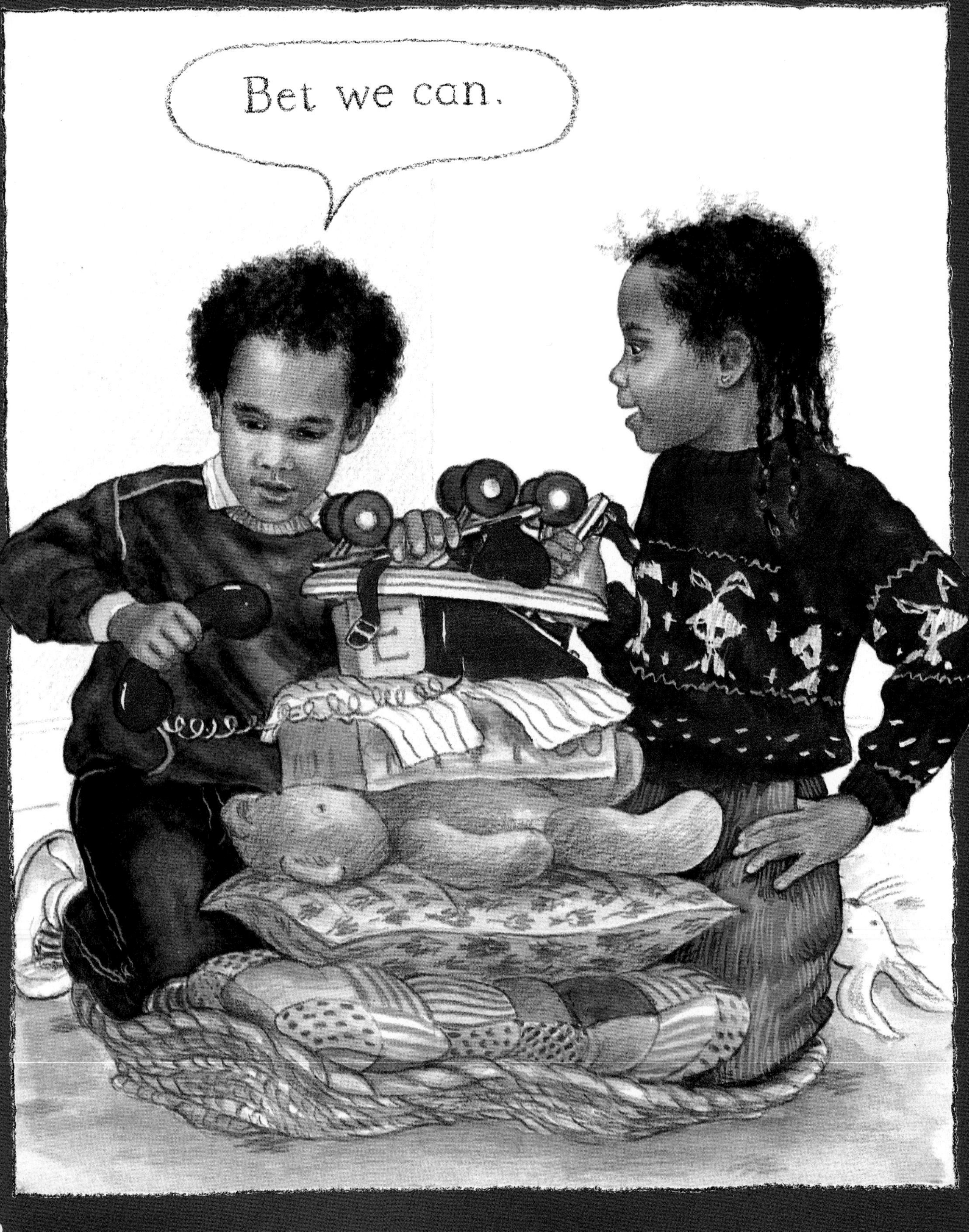
Bet we can.

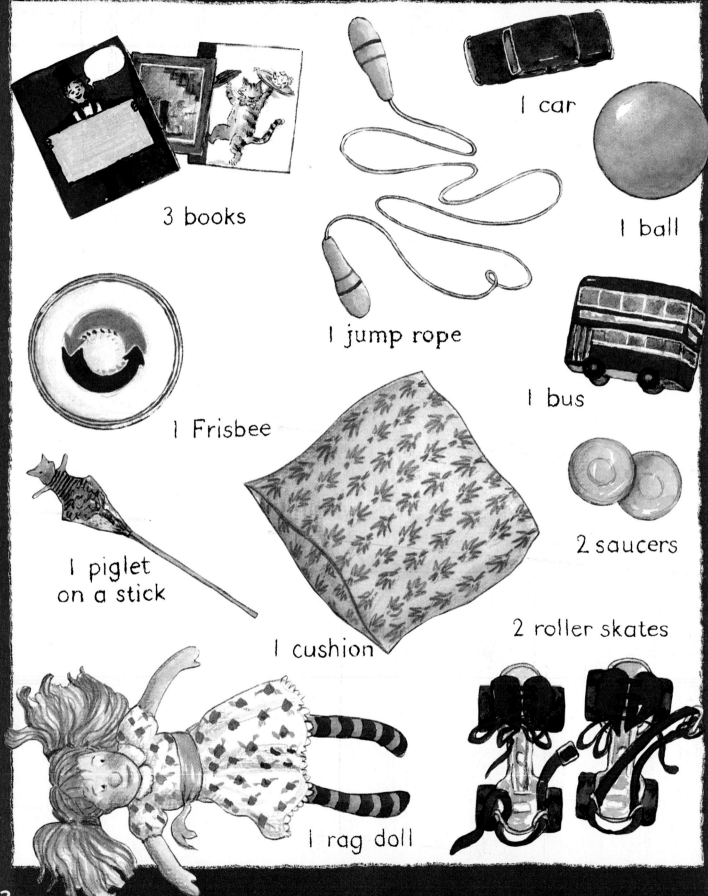

3 books

1 car

1 ball

1 jump rope

1 bus

1 Frisbee

2 saucers

1 piglet
on a stick

1 cushion

2 roller skates

1 rag doll

2 blocks

I ruler

I dress

I telephone

I yo-yo

I rabbit

2 cups

I quilt

I teddy bear

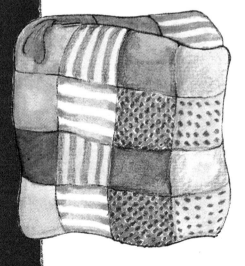

I jigsaw puzzle

I teapot

Read Together!

Beautiful Baskets

by Diane Hoyt-Goldsmith

My grandmother weaves Cherokee baskets.

- First she dips strips of cane in water to make them soft.

- Then she weaves the cane over and under, over and under.

- She shows me how she makes beautiful baskets.

Think About Reading

1. Finish the story map by filling in each blank.
   Write your answers on another piece of paper.
   Use the pictures as clues.

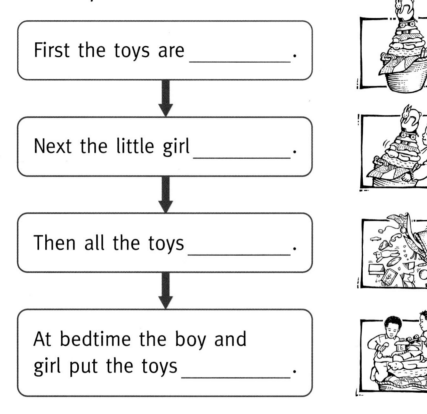

First the toys are _____.

↓

Next the little girl _____.

↓

Then all the toys _____.

↓

At bedtime the boy and
girl put the toys _____.

2. How are the children in <u>Bet You Can't</u> like
   the grandmother and granddaughter in
   "Beautiful Baskets"?

Write Speech Balloons

Draw a picture of a time when you helped someone do something. Include speech balloons with your picture.

Literature Circle

Both Bet You Can't and "Beautiful Baskets" tell about family members working together. What do you like about working with others?

Author/Illustrator
Penny Dale

Penny Dale is from England. When she writes a book, she begins with a large piece of paper. She draws 12 rectangles on the page. Each rectangle shows two pages in the layout of her book. She also uses sticky notes to make changes or to move her ideas around.

More Books by
Penny Dale

- All About Alice
- Rosie's Babies
- Ten Out of Bed

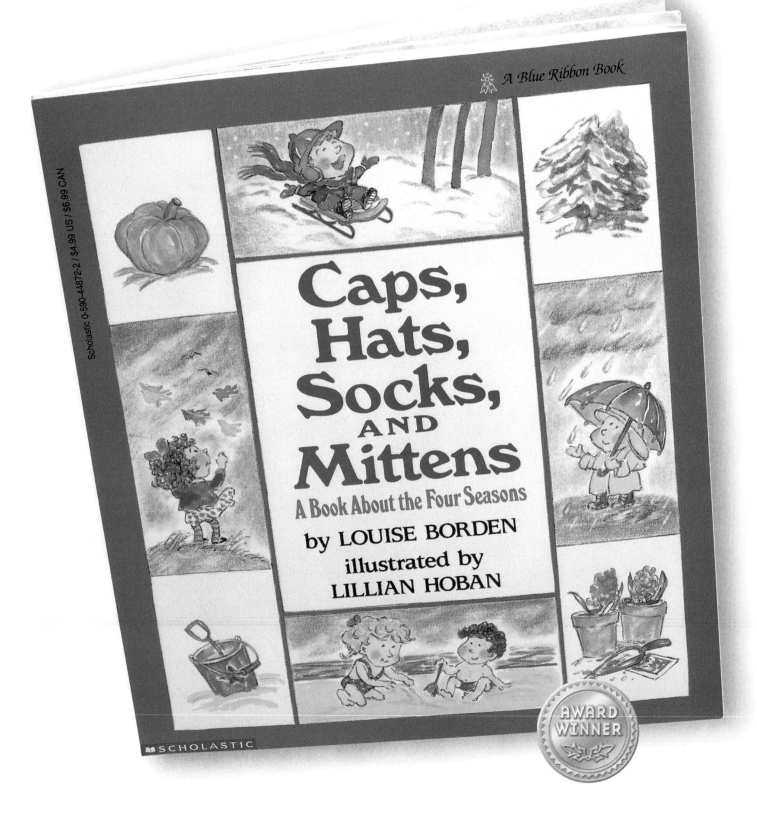

A Blue Ribbon Book

Scholastic 0-590-44872-2 / $4.99 US / $6.99 CAN

Caps, Hats, Socks, AND Mittens

A Book About the Four Seasons

by LOUISE BORDEN

illustrated by LILLIAN HOBAN

SCHOLASTIC

AWARD WINNER

Winter is
caps, hats,
socks,
and mittens.

Winter is
red sleds
up
a
hill.

Winter is
red sleds
down
a
hill.

Winter is
a lot of stuff to put on
and a lot of stuff
to get off!

Winter is fun
out and in.

Winter is
hot mugs
and hot cups.
Yum, yum.

Winter is

snug in bed.

Spring is
grass, grass, grass.
Dad cuts the grass
and cuts the grass
and cuts the grass.

Spring is mud to dig.

Mud on my hands.

Mud on my pants.

Mud in my pan.

Mud in my can.

A mud song!

Spring is
pots and plants
and plants in pots.

49

Spring is a nest of eggs,
a bed of twigs
and grass
and moss.

Spring is wet.

Drip, drip, drip.

Drip, drip, drip.

Spring is
picnics
in the sun.

Spring is
run, run, run!
Up, up, up!

Summer is
sun and sand,
flags and bands.

Summer is hot, hot, hot.

Lots of hot dogs.

Hot dog and hot dogs.

Summer is a ball game.

"I can bat."

"I can toss."

Caps off!

Hats off!

"I lost my mitt!"

Summer is . . .
"I can swim!"
"I can swim fast."
"1 . . . 2 . . . 3 . . ."
"Jump!"

Summer is
a jar full of bugs.

Summer is a fish in a pond
and a frog on a pad.

Fall is lots of smells.
Nuts and pumpkins
and corn in husks.

Fall is
red,
orange,
yellow,
brown
at dusk.

Fall is
pens and desks.

Last on the bus!
First off the bus!

Fall is
frost on the grass
before the sun is up.

Fall is soccer.
Soccer is fun.
We run.
We kick.
"Hands off the ball!"

Fall is black cats
and black hats
after the sun is down.

Then back to . . .
caps,
hats,
socks,
and mittens.

FOX CUBS

illustrated by Yoko Imoto

Read Together!

In the mountains, fox cubs play their dress-up game…
Crushed wildflowers color their cheeks
And fallen maple leaves adorn their hair.

In winter, the fox cubs can't play dress-up games…
The withered leaves are too dry to make a suit
And the pretty flowers have long since gone.

The cubs can't play any games back in their den…
Their tails are too fluffy now and just get in the way.
And so they wait restlessly…thinking about the coming spring.

Think About Reading

1. List some words from the story that tell about summer.

2. Why is this story called <u>Caps, Hats, Socks, and Mittens</u>?

3. What is your favorite season? Why?

4. What is this story about?

5. How do you think <u>Caps, Hats, Socks, and Mittens</u> and "Fox Cubs" are alike?

Write a Caption

Both <u>Caps, Hats, Socks, and Mittens</u> and "Fox Cubs" are about fun things to do during each season. Choose a season and draw a picture of something you do during it. Then write a sentence to go with your picture.

Literature Circle

The title <u>Caps, Hats, Socks, and Mittens</u> refers to the winter part of the story. What do you think the title might be for spring, summer, and fall?

Illustrator
Lillian Hoban

Lillian Hoban did many things in her life. She went to art school. She also studied and taught dance. When she had her third child, Ms. Hoban stopped dancing and began illustrating children's books.

More Books by
Lillian Hoban

- <u>Arthur's Loose Tooth</u>
- <u>Emmet Otter's Jug-Band Christmas</u>
- <u>Frances</u>

Soccer Is Our Game

adapted by
Wiley Blevins

Soccer is fun.

We like to play a lot.

We can't hit the ball with our hands.

We must kick it with our feet.

Our coach helps us.
She shows us how to kick.
She also shows us how to pass the ball.

We pass the ball with long kicks.

We can hit the ball with
our heads, too.
It is not easy.
We have to practice a lot.

73

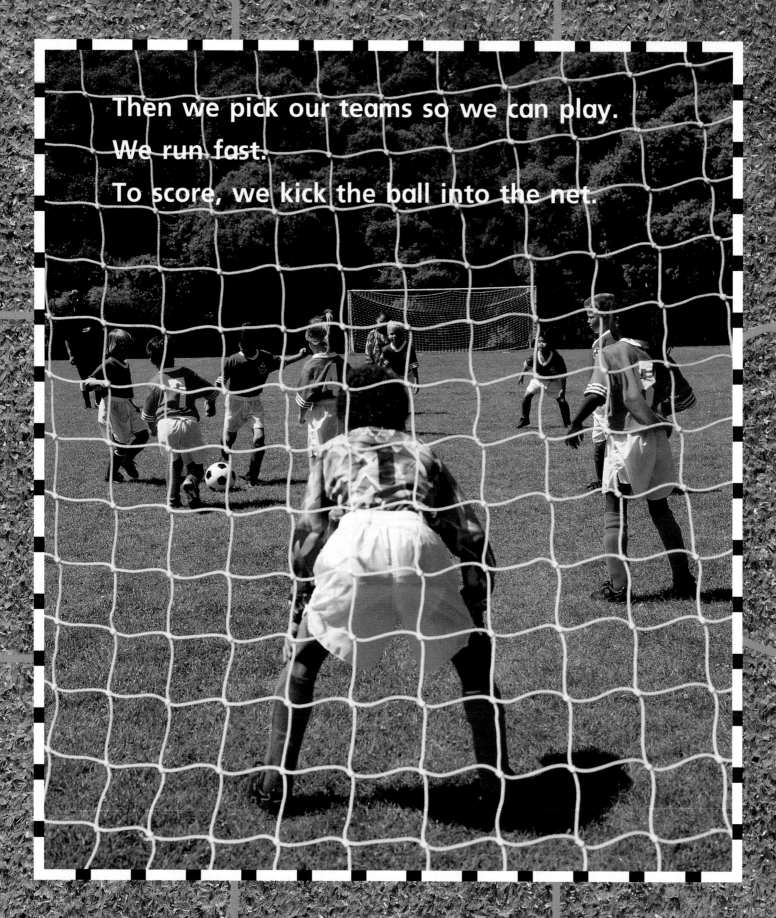

Then we pick our teams so we can play.

We run fast.

To score, we kick the ball into the net.

At halftime, we rest.
We always have a
good snack, too.
Then the coach yells
for us to play hard.

Soccer is not easy.
But we do our best to win.

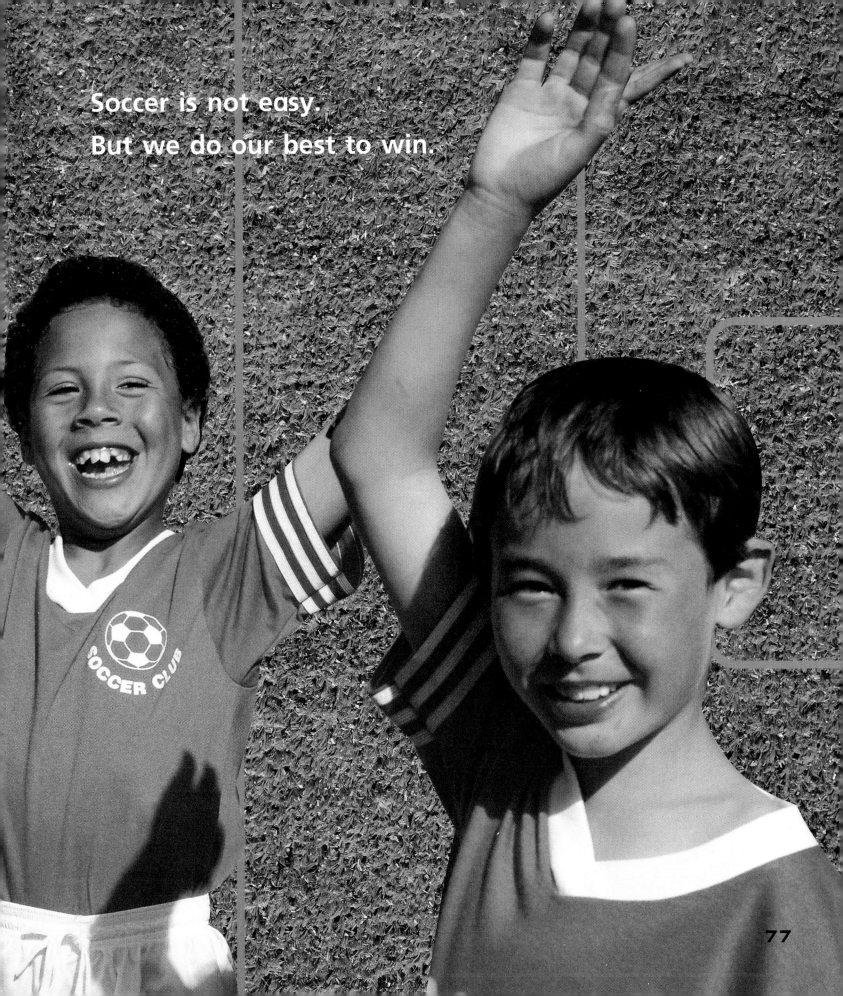

Win or lose, we have a lot of fun.
Soccer is our game!

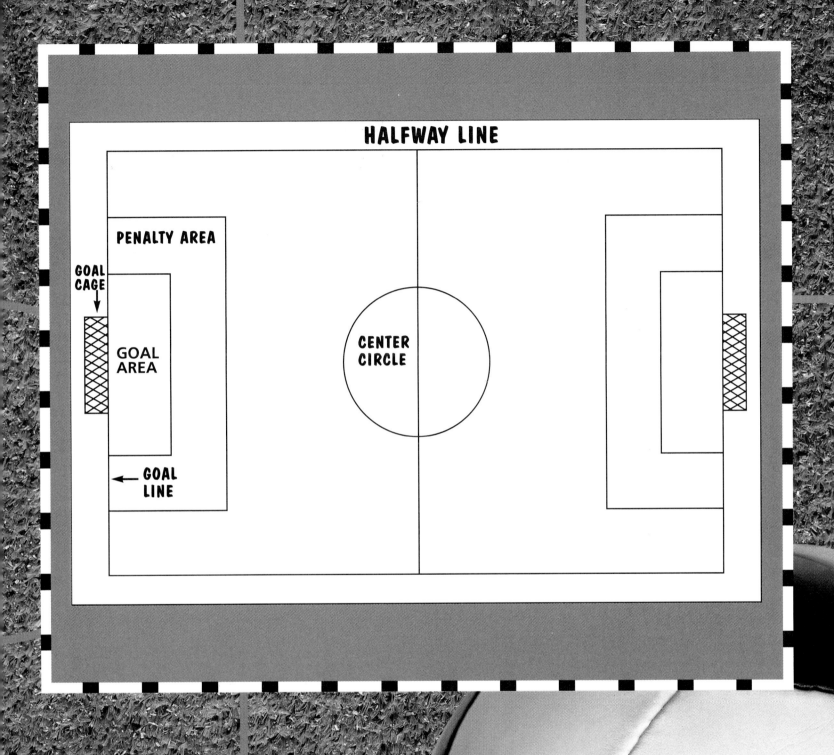

Read Together!

Danny Prenat
Soccer Coach

Danny Prenat coaches young people in Florida. He shows them how to work as a team.

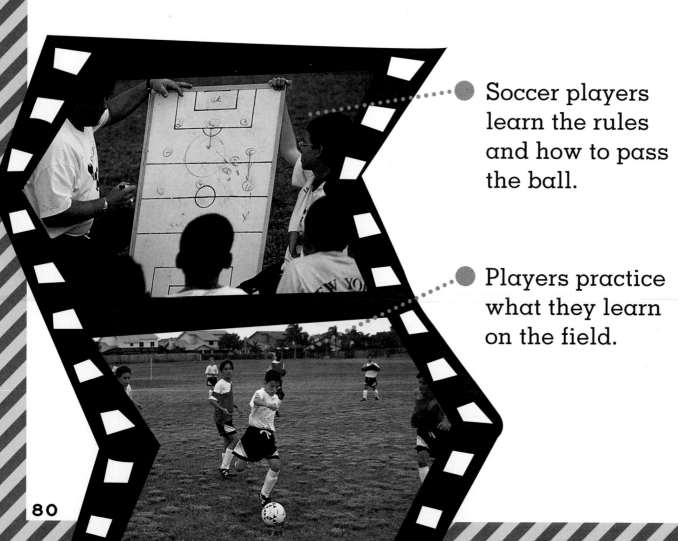

Soccer players learn the rules and how to pass the ball.

Players practice what they learn on the field.

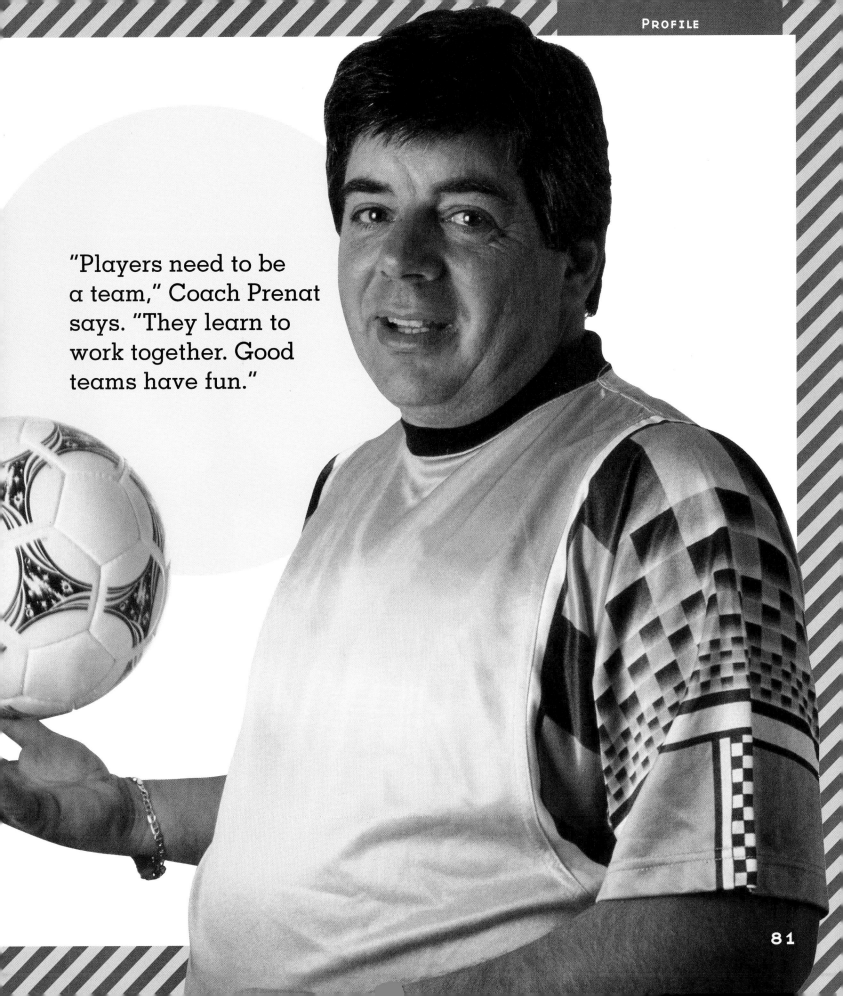

"Players need to be a team," Coach Prenat says. "They learn to work together. Good teams have fun."

81

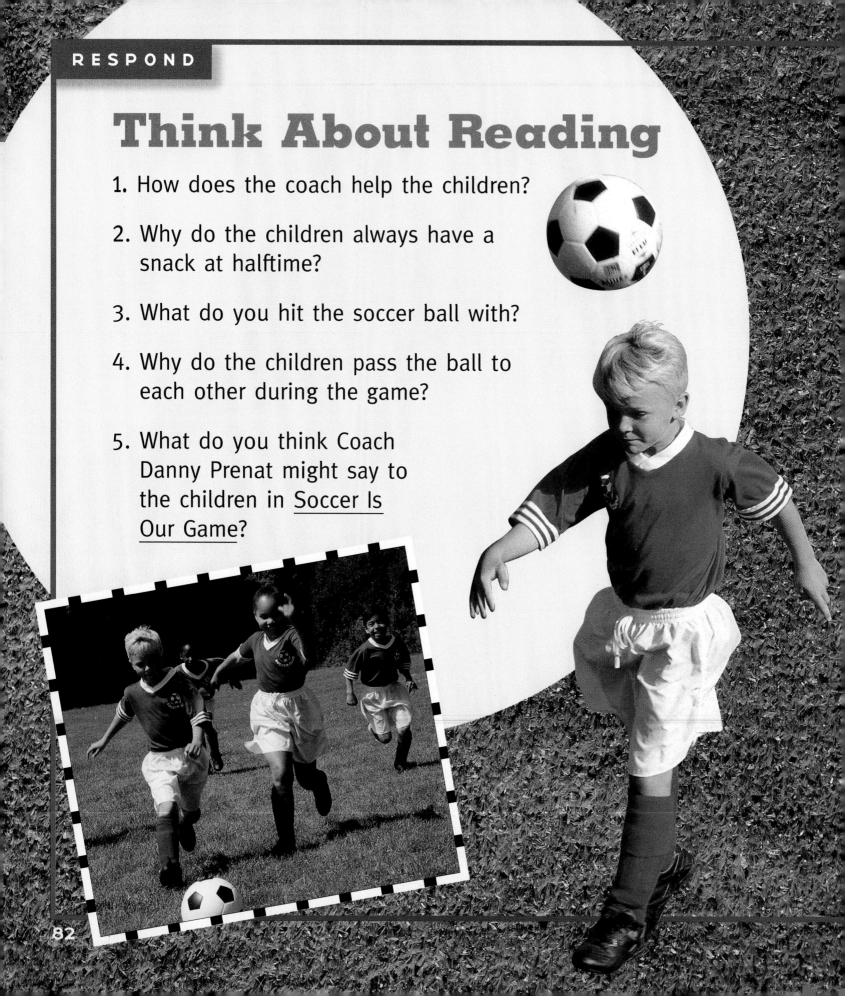

Think About Reading

1. How does the coach help the children?

2. Why do the children always have a snack at halftime?

3. What do you hit the soccer ball with?

4. Why do the children pass the ball to each other during the game?

5. What do you think Coach Danny Prenat might say to the children in <u>Soccer Is Our Game</u>?

Write a Caption

Draw a picture of a soccer game. Write a sentence to go with your picture. Tell a fact about your picture.

Literature Circle

What facts did you learn about soccer from the story? How did the photos help you learn these facts?

Author
Wiley Blevins

Wiley Blevins was an elementary school teacher. He now writes books for teachers and children. He is a big football and soccer fan. On weekends he likes to play sports.

More Books by
Wiley Blevins

- <u>Once Upon a Hill: An Appalachian Tale</u>
- <u>Whale of a Joke!</u>
- <u>Food</u>

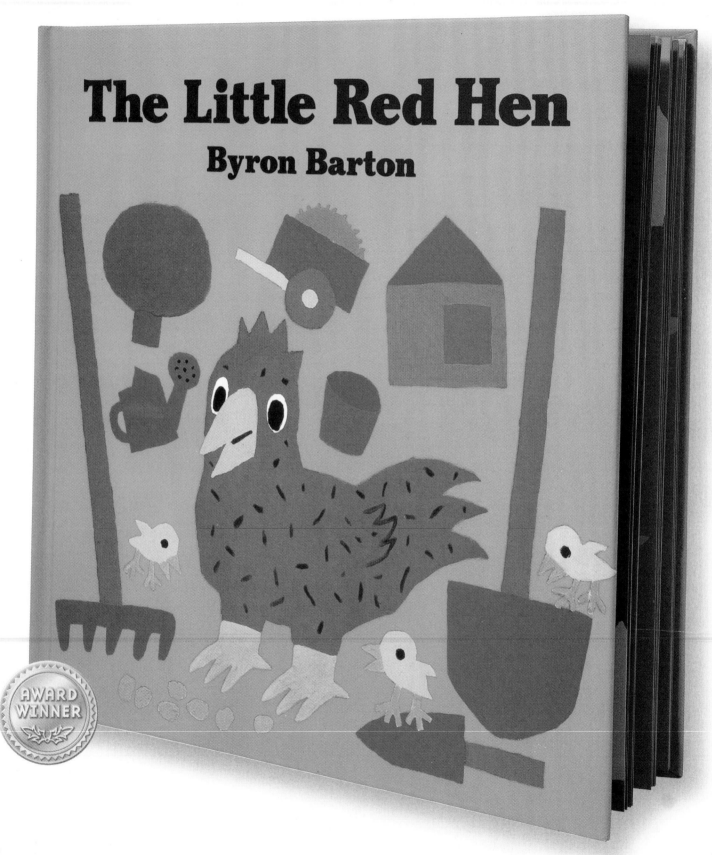

The Little Red Hen
Byron Barton

Once there were four friends—

a pig,   **a duck,**

a cat,   **and a little red hen.**

The little red hen had three baby chicks.

One day the little red hen was pecking in the ground,

and she found some seeds.

She went to her three friends and asked,
"Who will help me plant these seeds?"

88

"Not I," squealed the pig.
"Not I," quacked the duck.
"Not I," meowed the cat.

"Then I will plant the seeds," said the little red hen.
And she did.

And the seeds sprouted and grew into large stalks of wheat.

Then the little red hen asked her three friends,
"Who will help me cut these stalks of wheat?"

"Not I," meowed the cat.

"Not I," squealed the pig.

"Not I," quacked the duck.

"Then I will cut the wheat," said the little red hen.

And she did.

Then the little red hen asked her three friends,
"Who will help me thresh this wheat?"

"Not I," squealed the pig.   "Not I," quacked the duck.

"Not I," meowed the cat.

"Then I will thresh the wheat," said the little red hen.

And she did.

Then the little red hen asked her friends,
"Who will help me grind these grains of wheat into flour?"

"Not I," squealed the pig.
"Not I," quacked the duck.
"Not I," meowed the cat.

"Then I will grind the wheat into flour,"
said the little red hen.

And she did.

Then the little red hen asked her three friends,
"Who will help me make this flour into bread?"

"Not I," meowed the cat.

"Not I," squealed the pig.

"Not I," quacked the duck.

"Then I will make the flour into bread," she said.

And she did.

Then the little red hen called to her friends,

"Who will help me eat   this bread?"

"I will," quacked the duck.
"I will," meowed the cat.
"I will," squealed the pig.

"Oh no," said the little red hen.
"We will eat the bread."

And they did—

the little red hen and her three little chicks.

Quack! Quack! Quack!

illustrated by Marc Brown

    Five little ducks that I once knew,

Big ones, little ones, skinny ones, too.

But the one little duck with the

Feather on his back,

All he could do was, "Quack! Quack! Quack!"

All he could do was, "Quack! Quack! Quack!"

   Down to the river they would go,

Waddling, waddling, to and fro.

But the one little duck with the

Feather on his back,

All he could do was, "Quack! Quack! Quack!"

All he could do was, "Quack! Quack! Quack!"

Up from the river they would come.

 Ho, ho, ho, ho, hum, hum, hum.

 But the one little duck with the

Feather on his back,

 All he could do was, "Quack! Quack! Quack!"

All he could do was, "Quack! Quack! Quack!"

Think About Reading

Finish the story map by answering the questions.
Write the answers on another piece of paper.

Characters

1. Who are the four friends in
The Little Red Hen?

2. How many baby chicks does
the little red hen have?

Problem

3. What problem does the little
red hen have?

Ending

4. Since the little red hen's friends
wouldn't help her, who got to
eat the bread?

5. How are the little red hen and
the ducks in "Quack, Quack,
Quack" alike?

Write Speech Balloons

Draw a picture of The Little Red Hen. Make speech balloons to go with each character in your picture.

Literature Circle

Think about what might have happened in The Little Red Hen if the pig, duck, and cat had helped the little red hen. How would the story have been different?

Author/Illustrator
Byron Barton

Byron Barton has been writing and illustrating books for twenty years. He tries to use words and pictures that will help children read the story by themselves. Barton has won many awards for his popular books.

More Books by
Byron Barton

- Bones, Bones, Dinosaur Bones
- I Want to Be an Astronaut
- Three Bears

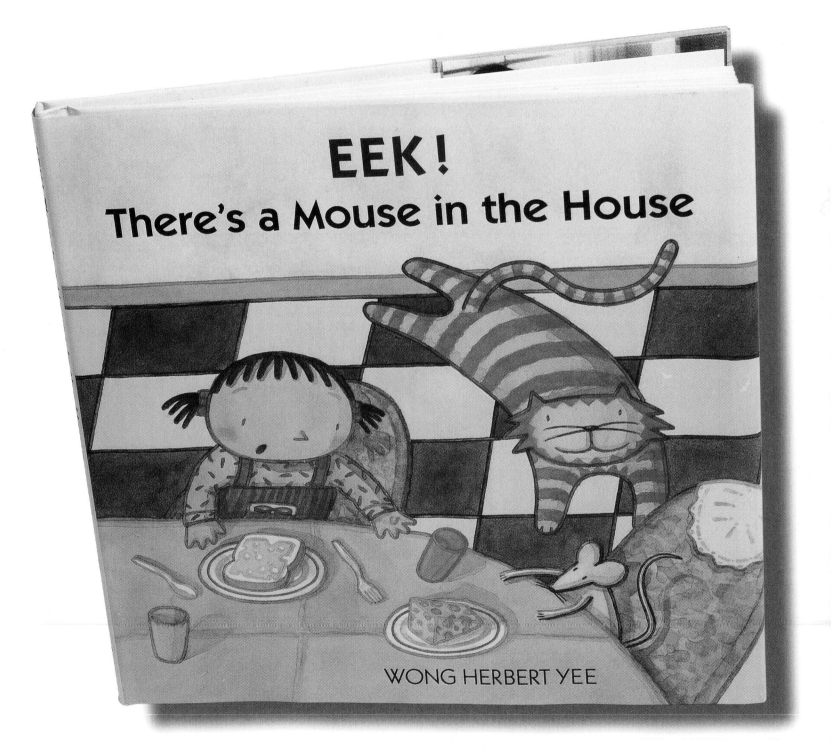

EEK!

There's a Mouse in the house.

Send in the Cat
to chase that rat!

Uh-oh!

The Cat knocked over a lamp.

Send in the Dog
to catch that scamp!

Dear me!

The Dog has broken a dish.

And now the Cat is after the fish.

Send in the Hog
to shoo that Dog!

Oh my!

The Hog is eating the cake.

Sending the Hog
was a big mistake.

Send in the Cow.

Send that Cow NOW!

Oh no!

The Cow is dancing
with a mop.

Send in the Sheep
to make her stop!

Goodness!

The Sheep is tangled
in yarn.

Send in the Hen
from the barn!

Mercy!

The Hen is laying eggs
on the table.

Send in the Horse
from the stable!

Heavens!

The Horse kicked a hole
in the wall.

Send in the Elephant
to get rid of them ALL!

The Elephant was BIG,
but he squeezed through the door.

Once he was in,
there was room for no more.

Out of the house marched
the Cat and the Cow.

Out came the Horse and
the Hen and the Hog.

Out walked the Sheep.

Out ran the Dog.

But then from within,
there came a shout:

EEK! There's a Mouse in the house!

Something BIG has been here

by Jack Prelutsky
illustrated by Jane Conteh-Morgan

Something big has been here,
what it was, I do not know,
for I did not see it coming,
and I did not see it go,
but I hope I never meet it,
if I do, I'm in a fix,
for it left behind its footprints,
they are size nine-fifty-six.

Think About Reading

1. Which animal first tried to get the mouse out of the house?

2. What scared the elephant?

3. Why do you think there is a piece of cheese on almost every page in the story?

4. How are the beginning and ending of the story alike?

5. How are EEK! There's a Mouse in the House and "Something Big Has Been Here" the same?

Write a Caption

Draw a picture of your favorite part of the story. Write a sentence to go with your picture. Tell a fact about your picture.

Literature Circle

What if "Something Big Has Been Here" was about a mouse? What would be the title of the poem? How would the poem change?

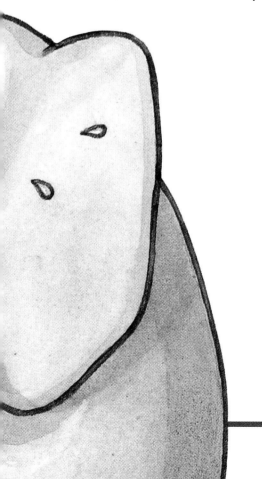

Author/Illustrator
Wong Herbert Yee

Wong Herbert Yee wrote EEK! There's a Mouse in the House for his daughter Ellen. When Yee saw a mouse in his house, he built a maze that ended at the front door. The mouse ran through the maze until it found itself outside.

More Books by
Wong Herbert Yee

- Mrs. Brown Went to Town
- Big Black Bear
- Fireman Small

WORD LIST

e

basket	pecking
bed	pens
best	red
bet	rest
desks	send
dress	sleds
eggs	smells
get	them
help	then
hen	thresh
left	well
let's	went
mittens	wet
nest	yells
net	

ck

back	pick
blocks	quack
chicks	snack
duck	socks
kick	stick
pecking	

g

big	grass
bugs	hog
dig	mugs
dog	pecking
doing	pig
eggs	piglet
flags	rag
frog	sending
get	snug
go	twigs

U

bugs	mugs
bus	must
cubs	nuts
cups	pumpkins
cut	run
duck	snug
dusk	stuff
fun	sun
hum	up
husks	us
jump	yum
mud	

Decodable Words

k

basket	kick
desks	pumpkins
dusk	stalks
husks	

y

yells	yum
yo-yo	

th

that	this
them	with
then	

q

quack	quilt
quacked	

x

fix	six
fox	

/z/s

bands	mittens
bugs	mugs
cubs	pens
eggs	pumpkins
flags	sleds
hands	smells
has	twigs
is	

sh

dish	thresh
fish	

v

five	visit
river	

High-Frequency Words

are	from	me	put
asked	has	now	through
before	how	off	too
came	into	or	up
first	little	our	why

Acknowledgments

Grateful acknowledgment is made to the following sources for permission to reprint from previously published material. The publisher has made diligent efforts to trace the ownership of all copyrighted material in this volume and believes that all necessary permissions have been secured. If any errors or omissions have inadvertently been made, proper corrections will gladly be made in future editions.

"Bet You Can't" from BET YOU CAN'T by Penny Dale. Copyright © 1988 by Penny Dale. Reprinted by permission of Candlewick Press.

"Caps, Hats, Socks, and Mittens" from CAPS, HATS, SOCKS, AND MITTENS by Louise Borden, illustrated by Lillian Hoban. Text copyright © 1989 by Louise W. Borden. Illustrations copyright © 1989 by Lillian Hoban. Reprinted by permission of Scholastic Inc.

"Fox Cubs" by Yoshio Katsu from BEST-LOVED CHILDREN'S SONGS FROM JAPAN by Yoko Imoto. Originally published in Japan by Kodansha Ltd. English translation copyright © 1996 by Heian International, Inc. Reprinted by permission of Heian International, Inc.

"Soccer Is Our Game" from SOCCER IS OUR GAME by Leila B. Gemme, adapted by Wiley Blevins. Copyright © 1979 by Regensteiner Enterprises, Inc. Text adaptation copyright © 2000 by Scholastic Inc. Adapted by permission of Children's Press, Chicago.

"The Little Red Hen" from THE LITTLE RED HEN by Byron Barton. Copyright © 1993 by Byron Barton. Reprinted by permission of HarperCollins Publishers.

"Quack! Quack! Quack!" from HAND RHYMES by Marc Brown. Copyright © 1985 by Marc Brown. Reprinted by permission of Dutton Children's Books, a division of Penguin Putnam Inc.

EEK! THERE'S A MOUSE IN THE HOUSE by Wong Herbert Yee. Copyright © 1992 by Wong Herbert Yee. Reprinted by permission of Houghton Mifflin Company. All rights reserved.

"Something Big Has Been Here" from SOMETHING BIG HAS BEEN HERE by Jack Prelutsky. Text copyright © 1990 by Jack Prelutsky. By permission of Greenwillow Books, a division of William Morrow & Company, Inc.

Photography and Illustration Credits

Photos: p. 2br, 70–78, 82, 83, Grant Huntington for Scholastic Inc.; pp. 4–5, 80ml, Maryellen Baker for Scholastic Inc.; p. 35, © Lawrence Migdale; pp. 70–71bg, 70bl, 72–73bg, 74–75bg, 76–77bg, 78–79bg, Halley Ganges for Scholastic Inc.; p. 70bc, Nicole Katano for Scholastic Inc.; p. 71c, Ana Nance for Scholastic Inc.; pp. 80–81, Tony Savino for Scholastic Inc.; p. 83, Moya McAllister for Scholastic Inc.; p. 141, Houghton Mifflin.

Design/Production: Dinardo Design

Cover: Arthur Tilley/FPG International

Back Cover: Jim West

Illustrations: p. 36: Ruth Flannigan for Scholastic Inc.; p. 139: Jane Conteh-Morgan

Illustrated Author Photos: pp. 37, 115, 141, 83, 69: Gabe DiFiore for Scholastic Inc.